The Insider Railroad Jobs Guide

Photo courtesy of
Ronald Kappel ~ passed 2015

1

The Insider Railroads Job Guide

Table of Contents

Photo courtesy of
Susan Thomas ~ http://community.webshots.com/user/susan526

Disclaimer: This book and website is not affiliated with any railroad company, trade school or website listed herein.

Introduction

Congratulations on your wise purchase of my book on how to get a job in the railroad industry and make up to $75,000 per year. This figure is not make believe, as you can go right now to: https://jobs.bnsf.com/search/?q= and see for yourself. Conductors start at about $70k per year for the first two years then goes up from there!

Click on "Conductor Trainee" and you will see positions advertising from $70,000 to $82,000 per year achievable income.

The exact wording is **"average annual salary of $70,000 - $82,000."**

This particular website belongs to BNSF which is a Class One railroad. All of the **Class One railroads pay just about the same amount of money**. Most of them are represented by the same unions. We will take a closer look at the different railroads later on in this book.

Beware: Websites constantly change web pages and links so some links may not work, simply **search on the website**.

The reason I wrote this book is so that you can learn from my mistakes and experience in getting hired with a Class One railroad.

When I went to my first railroad interview there were over 90 different men and women there, all applying for the same job which was Conductor. The problem was they were only hiring about 7 people.

Needless to say I did not get hired at that interview. However, I was able to learn from that interview process. I found out what I needed to say and do in order to get hired the next time I interviewed with a railroad company.

This book will explain everything I learned and did in order to get hired. If you think it's easy getting hired with the railroad you are mistaken. They are very picky and one wrong word or admission will ruin your chances.

This book will give you the **secrets, tips and advice** to greatly **increase your chances** of getting hired.

Best Regards,

Sean Martin

Chapter 1

You might be wondering why I did not get hired at my first interview with a railroad company. I made one big mistake and that automatically, in the interviewers opinion, blew any chance I had at getting hired at that particular time.

What was it? He asked me if I would rather work in a different location, owned by the same railroad, and I said "yes." What he was doing was testing me because **I was not from the area that I was interviewing in!**

He wanted to see if I was going to transfer to another location once I got hired and finished the training program. Of course he did not want to hire someone and then have them transfer out of his terminal once that person got trained to do his or her job. Rightly so, from his perspective as a manager.

I answered yes to his question and that was all it took to finish my interview and **NOT get the job**. Regardless of any positive traits or characteristics I had on my resume, I was not going to get hired once I admitted to preferring to work at a different railroad terminal.

This is what I mean when I say that one wrong answer or word will get your interview process finished quicker than you can snap your briefcase back shut.

Let's talk about some of the things that will automatically prevent you from being hired at any railroad company:

- If you have had a felony in the past 7 years
- If you have had a DUI (driving while intoxicated) in the past 2-3 years
- If you are physically impaired it will bar you from certain positions
- If you can not pass a physical such as a Department of Transportation physical
- If you do not pass their written exams or physical test
- If you can not pass a drug test either by urine or hair testing
- If you are color blind you will be eliminated from positions such as Conductor
- If you can not pass a background investigation
- If you smell like cigarette smoke, they avoid hiring smokers

I mention these up front because if for example, your were arrested and convicted for a felony last year you might as well **not even waste your time applying** for a job with the railroad industry.

The same goes for drugs. If you are using drugs, don't even bother applying because they will find it in your urine or your hair. Do not think you can fool the drug test because they are very sophisticated. Needless to say if you are a drug user, other railroaders will not want to work with you because the job is dangerous and your life is in other people's hands all the time.

As far as the written and physical tests that the railroads give you, only by participating in them will you know if you can pass them or not.

Every railroad gives you different written exams and some give you a physical test while you are at the interview. For example, Union Pacific, if you are applying for Train Service (Conductor), will give you a grip test, sit-up test and a strength test measuring your ability to pull in an upwards position with your arms.

The Union Pacific's written test consists of a reading comprehension test which is **not very difficult to pass**.

Burlington Northern Santa Fe (BNSF) does not give you any physical test at the interview process. However all railroads will require you to pass a detailed and exhaustive physical performed by a medical doctor.

BNSF will give you numerous written tests. One is a personality type test that is really just a pass or fail test. They basically are looking for you to make a decision such as "strongly agree" or "strongly disagree." If you answer a lot of the questions "in-between" then you will fail.

They also will quiz you on math percentages, adding, subtracting and they will ask you **several safety-related questions**.

All of these pre-interview tests are not very hard and from what I have seen and experienced, about 95% of everyone who takes them passes. So **don't stress out over them**. All of the railroad companies give the same type of pre-interview test.

Another thing to think about before you try to get a railroad job is if you really want to work in the conditions that the railroad will require you to work in. What I am referring to is what is called the "scary speech."

The scary speech is a speech that every railroad will give you at every hiring session. The **purpose is to weed out those people who do not want to work in the conditions** that are required by the railroad industry.

What I mean is that when you work for the railroad, pretty much every single job is shift work, 24 hours a day, 365 days a year. The railroad never stops. Not for holidays, rain, hail, sleet or snow. So if you are one of those people who does not ever want to work night shift, for example, then the railroad is not for you.

If you want weekends off, then the railroad is not for you.

If you want regular hours the railroad is not for you.

If you want Christmas and New Years off every year, the railroad is not for you.

If you are applying for a Conductor position, then you will basically be gone every other day/night from your family. If you can't handle that, then the railroad is not for you.

If you don't want to work outside in all kinds of weather conditions, then the railroad is not for you.

Like I said before, the railroad is a non-stop business **365 days a year, 24 hours a day**. It's more of a lifestyle than anything else. I tell you this upfront because if you understand what is required now and the requirements don't agree with you, then this will save you a bunch of wasted time and energy.

That is basically the gist of the scary speech. Many people come to hiring sessions for the railroad and don't understand how the railroad operates. The speech gives people a **chance to leave if they know they don't want to work** under those conditions.

Not every job with the railroad requires you to travel or be away from home. If you're applying for a diesel mechanic, for example, then you will work one of the shifts in a 24 hour day. Everything in the railroad industry is also governed by seniority. At the beginning you will not have enough seniority to hold a day shift for example. So you will most likely be working the night shift and the longer you work for the company you will gain seniority and someday will have enough of it to bid on a day shift.

The good news is that if you don't mind the conditions I listed above, the railroad industry can provide you with a **very nice income along with great retirement and benefits.**

Now that we have that out of the way and if you're still with me then let's get on with what you need to know in order to get that railroad job!

Photo courtesy of

Rob Jacox ~ http://www.trainweb.org/westernrails/

Chapter 2

The first thing you need to know is, the #1 subject every railroad company is concerned about and looking for in every candidate is **SAFETY!**

They want people who can function in a safe manner and perform their job without getting injured or doing something stupid that is going to get them or others hurt.

We will talk about the interview process later on but safety is one of the main things you want to mention during your interview. One of the best things you can do right now if you are employed is to **start a safety committee at your work place!** I know it sounds corny but it is very impressive to have on your resume as well as being able to mention it during your interview.

It's as simple as going to your boss at work and telling him or her that you want to start a safety committee to ensure that employees at work are performing in a safe manner and that the workplace itself is set up in a safe work environment.

Your safety committee does not have to include any other persons it could be just you. Go around your workplace and do an inspection for any unsafe work conditions such as exposed loose electrical wiring, fire extinguishers updated and in proper working order, etc…

Congratulations! You are now the new Safety Coordinator for your company!

You can now add this very **impressive title to your resume** and let your future railroad employer know that you are the Safety Coordinator for your company.

This really impresses railroad managers because they love to hire people who are safety minded and have taken the bull by the horns and actually did something about it in their past employment.

The second most important trait railroad employers are looking for is **stability in past employment.** They love people who have been at their present employer for five, ten or fifteen years. The railroad is going to spend a great deal of money training you for your job and the last thing they want is for that person to quit after six or twelve months.

This is why they like to see stability. If you can show good stability then you have half the battle won in being hired. If on the other hand, you have had numerous jobs, then you will be behind the eight ball; however do not despair.

I am going to show you later on in this book how to counter that problem. It involves trade schools.

The third most important trait railroad employers are looking for has to do with **experience working shift work**. Because as I mentioned before, almost all the jobs are shift work and they want people who have worked shift work before.

Many people do not like shift work and the last thing they want is someone to quit after getting trained because that employee found out that they do not like working different shifts.

Most likely they will ask you during the interview, "Have you worked shift work before?" Luckily for me in the past I did work shift work before so I could truthfully answer "yes." I would never encourage anyone to lie during their interview process. Therefore if you have never worked shift work before, ask your boss to let you do some so that you can answer truthfully.

Shift work is a big factor in their decision making so you want to make sure that you can answer that question with a "yes." This is why railroads love people who are coming from jobs such as mill workers, prisons, hospitals, or any job where everyone works different shifts.

The above is what I refer to as the big three "**S's**", **Safety, Stability** and **Shift** work. If you have all three, then you are going to have a big advantage over the other candidates.

Those three items cover our discussion on your past performance and abilities. The only one you really don't have any control over is the stability if you have hopped around from job to job in a short period of time.

However, later on we will deal with how to overcome that in the best possible way.

Generally speaking, there are two different ways to get hired on with a railroad company. The **first one is to get hired on directly** with a railroad company by going to their website and filling out the application and waiting to get a notice to show up for the interview.

The **second way is to go through a trade school** specializing in the railroad industry. We will discuss trade schools later in this book.

After we discuss the interview process we will learn where to go to find the websites of different railroad companies as well as how to find the jobs.

Chapter 3

So far we have learned what the railroad companies are looking for as far as our past experience and what to do in order to improve our chances of getting hired in respect to our past experience.

Now we are going to discuss the interview process and learn what kinds of questions they will be asking you and what are the appropriate responses.

The interview process usually takes place in a large conference room of a local hotel in the city where the interview is being held. You will see lots of other candidates there waiting to go through the interview process just like you.

Many will be wearing jeans, t-shirts, baseball caps and boots. **DO NOT make this mistake of dressing so casually.** It shows disrespect to the people doing the interview and makes the person look like an idiot.

Many times one of the interviewers from the railroad will be a woman. Women interviewers are not impressed by people showing up in jeans and a baseball cap. You should wear slacks and a nice collar shirt with dress shoes. I suggest a tie but that is just me. If you have tattoos on your arms then make sure you wear a long sleeve shirt. Do not wear any type of hat!

Be low key and prepared. If they tell you to bring anything to the interview with you such as driver's license, SSN card, pencils, pens, copy of application, resume, etc…, **make sure you have everything!**

One interview I was at, a guy got kicked out because he did not have a copy of his application they had requested him to bring. Another guy showed up 2 minutes late and was told he could not interview because he was late.

Show up at least 15 minutes early. The first thing they will do is have all the candidates take any written test the company wants you to take. After this they will have you do any physical test they want you to perform.

For those candidates that pass those first tests, they will be granted an interview. The best advice I can give you for your interview is to **be prepared.**

You must anticipate the questions they are going to ask you and have your answer ready with out having to think about it. Always answer, "Yes sir" or "No ma'am" when answering questions. This shows respect and the quickest way not to get hired is to make them think you have an attitude. **Be humble yet assertive at the same time.**

I am going to list some typical questions they will ask you during the hiring interview. Try to commit these questions and answers to memory because they could mean the difference between getting hired and not getting hired.

1. What are 3 reasons why "ABC" railroad should hire you?

a) I am a worker with safety in mind and am team oriented. Safety and teamwork go hand in hand. I also have experience in safety as I am the Safety Coordinator for my current employer.

b) I am a "guarantee employee." What I mean by that is I have done a great deal of research on the railroad industry before I decided to make a career change. I know what all is involved and you don't have to worry about me quitting after getting hired and trained because I know what the job involves.

Side note: Many people quit after getting hired with the railroad because they find out they don't like the job or working shift work etc... The above answer is designed to "calm any fears" they have of that.

c) I am a very good employee. I never call in sick and I like to work overtime. I also want to advance in my career and I know that "ABC" railroad will allow me that opportunity. I also have a lot of direct experience such as safety, mechanical, (fill in the blanks) that relate directly to this job.

2. What are 3 reasons you want to work for "ABC" railroad?

a) I want a career and not just a job. ABC railroad is the best railroad and will provide me with the best opportunity to use my skills and allow me to advance and grow within the company.

b) ABC railroad is dedicated to safety. I am a worker with safety in mind as a top priority and I am team oriented. Last year ABC railroad spent xxxx dollars on safety improvement and I want to be with a company that is safety oriented.
(This is where you want to add something about the company that is positive that you were able to find out by doing research on their company website.)

c) ABC railroad is a 100% solid company. Your profits are up 7% over last year. The company is in a solid growth mode and I want to be with a railroad company that is growing and not stagnant.
(This is where you want to add something about the company that is positive that you were able to find out by doing research on their company website.)

3. If you caught your boss stealing what would you do?

I would speak with his immediate supervisor and tell him or her that I witnessed my boss stealing.

4. **I see that you're not from this area. Are you and your family going to like living here?**

Yes, my wife and I are looking forward to the change and we like this area. I like the fact that there are lots of different fishing areas or this is a great area to raise kids in, etc... You have to think of a positive for that area.

5. **You realize that this job requires you to be away from home a lot. How will that affect you and your family?**

Actually it works in my favor because I am finishing my college degree and it will allow me to work on my laptop when I am away from home.
(You have to turn this question into a positive like I did above)

6. **There is a great deal of learning and bookwork when you are going through your training. Are you going to be able to pass and handle the studying?**

Yes, I found that when I am in a school environment, as long as I study the material I always score high on the test.

7. **Have you ever worked outside in extreme weather conditions?**

Yes I have. I actually prefer to work outside regardless of the weather rather than being inside manning a desk.

8. What do you feel is your strongest asset?

I feel my strongest asset is probably the fact that I am a very safe and hard working, reliable employee.

9. Have you ever been disciplined at work and if so what was it for?

Actually I have never been in trouble at work. I always do my job and help others.

These are some sample questions that you may very well be asked. The one thing you want to do is gear your interview to the railroad company to which you are applying.

The way to do that is to go to their website and look at the company history and financial information they have listed. **Anytime you can weave into your answer a quote or information from that company's background it shows that you have done your homework and places you a step above your competitors** i.e. the other candidates.

While I am on the subject of interviews, never volunteer any information that is derogatory. I know one guy who was asked if he had ever been disciplined at work before and he told them he had been.

He was disciplined for calling in sick too many times. He explained it was because his wife was sick and he needed to stay home to take care of the kids. Obviously he did not get hired!

Employers are not interested in excuses, only results. If you're not bright enough to hire a babysitter in the above situation, then you certainly are not bright enough for the company to give a job offer.

As fair or unfair as it may seem, most people who get jobs, get them because they told the company what they wanted to hear. Remember that statement and you will do a lot better on your interviews.

Remember to **act professionally and be humble**. Research the railroad company you are applying for and gear your answers towards that company.

If the company is the largest railroad company, mention during your interview that you want to work for the largest and best railroad company because they will offer the best opportunity for advancement.

If the railroad company is small, mention the fact that you prefer to work for a small railroad company because you feel it will be more career oriented and you will be able to take on more responsibility within a smaller company.

Do you get my drift? **Gear your interview to the company you are interviewing with. This will greatly increase your chances of getting hired.** Always turn every question into a positive!

In the next chapter we are going to talk about the background investigation and your application. These are very important so make sure you pay close attention!

Photo courtesy of
Rob Jacox ~ http://www.trainweb.org/westernrails/

Chapter 4

Let's talk about the application you are going to fill out. Most railroad companies will have you fill out an application online via their website.

The applications are all pretty much the same. They will ask your personal information, education, criminal history, and employment history.

For employment information they will want to know your last employers for 7-10 years previous, as well as the employers' phone number, address, and reason for leaving. They will also want the exact dates of past employment.

If you have had several jobs in the past then this is **going to require you to do some research and call your previous employers in order to get the exact dates you worked for them**. They are very picky on the dates so make sure you find out what they are.

When you are on the company website filling out the application make sure you have all the information I listed handy. The reason is because many of the websites have timers on them and if you don't finish the application in the required time, then the information will not be saved and you will end up having to re-do the entire application. I don't have to tell you what a drag that is…

Make sure you fill out the application right the first time. Some companies do not let you go back and edit the application after you submit it. This of course is very frustrating if you did not do the application right.

BNSF, last I checked, does allow you to go back and edit your application. All the railroads change this policy so each one is different.

The Background Investigation

The background investigation screws a lot of applicants up because they lie and then get caught. Once you lie on your application and they do a background investigation and find out something you left out or lied about you will automatically be disqualified for employment.

This is why the background investigation is so critical. You either pass it or you fail. Here are some of the things they will be investigating and checking:

    ✓ Your personal information such as your social security number.

    ✓ Some check your credit information and credit history.

    ✓ They will verify your educational information you told them, degrees etc…

✓ They will run a criminal check and verify that information.

✓ They will check your past employment information and verify your work history.

People always want to know what they can get away with and what they can't.

Basically in a nutshell it's this: Anything that is public record they can and will find out. Such as past arrest, educational information, driver license record, etc…

Therefore **do not lie on your application!** In preparing this book I did a lot of research, on top of actually going thru the entire hiring process myself. I found out that the most common question asked by job applicants is whether or not they should admit to getting fired or terminated from a former employer.

This is a tricky question and I will answer it by saying I would never tell anyone to lie on an application. Thankfully I did not have to lie in order to get hired with my railroad employer but I realize that other people feel they may have to in order to get a job.

Just because you got terminated from a past employer is not going to bar you from getting hired. The real question is, "What did you get fired for?"

If it was for something minor then don't worry about it. However there are some things that employers just simply will not hire a candidate for if they find out.

What I mean is if you did something stupid like punch your former boss in the face then not too many companies are going to want to hire you. If you admit to this then you **might as well go straight to the unemployment line.**

During the background investigation they will call your past employers and ask them the dates of your employment and why you left the company. Now here is the good news. **Most employers do not give out information on past employees except for the dates they were employed**. When asked why the employee left, they simply say that information is not available or that they do not give that information out.

This is good news for people who screwed up at a former employer. It's also possible they were a good employee but for whatever reason their last supervisor felt threatened by them and got them terminated for a bogus or false reason.

If you feel that you would not be hired because you were terminated by a former employer, you need to find out if that past employer gives out information on reasons past employees left the company.

Some companies even outsource their employment information so when companies or background investigators call to verify employment they never talk to a real person only a machine.

They punch in the applicant's social security number and get a recording listing their dates of employment and that is it. More and more companies are doing this for fear of being sued in court by a former employee.

So, getting back to the original question; **should you admit to getting fired for something really serious** i.e. "punching your former boss in the face," I would say it depends on weather or not your former employer gives out, "reason for leaving the company" information.

If you put on your application that you "quit" that job, then chances are slim that your future employer will find out anything different. This is if the former employer does not give out that information.

Again, I am not advising you to lie on your application I am only letting you know that many companies do not give out "reason for leaving company" information to future employers.

You must choose how you're going to use this information. Remember to **never lie about your public information** because they will easily find out everything about your educational, criminal and drivers license information.

Another thing to remember is when you put down that you quit a former job, you want to put down **a reason for quitting such as: "Quit for advancement with ABC Company."**

In our next chapter we are going to discuss railroad related trade schools and you do not want to skip this chapter because it can be very beneficial to attend a trade school appropriate for the craft in which you want to get hired.

Chapter 5

In this chapter I want to speak with you about trade schools. There are trade schools that specialize in different occupational specialties such as conductor, locomotive engineer, signal persons, dispatcher, maintenance of way, railroad security, etc...

Do you remember in a previous chapter I told you that if you had numerous jobs and did not have a lot of stability that I would show you how to get around that?

Well, trade schools are the answer. **A trade school can make up for a scattered background.** Trade schools are going to cost you a financial commitment on your part and the railroads know this.

When you decide to put yourself through a railroad trade school it shows that you are **committed to starting a new career and 100% serious about it.** This is a major plus on your resume and can "practically" guarantee you getting hired.

There are two basic ways to get hired on with one of the railroad companies. One is that is you get hired directly by the company via filling out an application with them and interviewing and getting the job.

The second way is via a trade school. Many of the trade schools are sponsored in part by a railroad company or **they set up interviews with a railroad company at the end of your schooling.**

If you have a solid background such as a long-term job, stability, and some safety experience such as I explained in an earlier chapter then you have a very good chance of getting hired if you read this book.

However, if you do not have great stability then you will seriously want to consider attending a railroad trade school. The **great benefit of attending a trade school is that if you go to the right one you can have a job offer within one week** of finishing the school and sometimes before you finish the trade school.

I am a big believer in trade schools because the chances of you getting a job right after the school are very, very good. Employers love to see applicants who went through a railroad trade school.

They already have a huge head start over everyone else hired because they have already studied and learned a great deal of what the railroad is going to teach you anyway.

Every trade school is going to charge you money to attend. Some are more expensive than others, but usually you can get a student loan for any school you wish to attend.

The main thing you want to find out about a trade school is **whether or not they get you a job interview with a railroad company** at the end of the school. The reason I say this is because you could be leaving that school with a job offer and that is a lot easier than going to a bunch of company websites and filling out applications waiting for them to call or email you with an appointment date.

The whole goal of going to a railroad trade school is to get hired with a railroad company. **If a trade school does not have any kind of job placement assistance then don't waste your time** at that school.

The only drawback to the job placement assistance that the trade schools offer is that you really do not have much of a choice as to where you will be employed. This is if you interview and want to be hired by that trade school's sponsoring railroad company.

For example if you attend the National Academy of Railroad Science in Kansas (the one I graduated from), they guarantee you an interview with Burlington Northern Santa Fe Railroad before your schooling is finished. Basically BNSF will offer you 2-5 different locations as to where you would like to work. Call to verify this, as situations are always fluid and may change!

If you pass the interview, background investigation and physical then you will be offered a job in one of those locations. They also require you to pass the trade school final exam with a score of 90% or better in order to be considered for employment with BNSF.

I am going to give you the website address of the different trade schools I have found while doing my research for this book. One thing to remember is that many trade schools offer discounts to people who live in the same state or city as the trade school location.

Please keep in mind that these links may change because schools change or cancel programs! Due to recent union contracts some schools are no longer doing the training for CSX Railroad. They are now doing their own training.

1. http://www.narstraining.com/
National Academy of Railroad Sciences (NARS) is located at Johnson County Community College in Overland Park, KS. The school is affiliated with BNSF railroad and taught by BNSF railroad employees. They offer training programs in Conductor training, Locomotive Engineer training, Signal training, Maintenance training, Mechanical and Telecom training.

The NARS program use to guarantee an interview with Burlington Northern Santa Fe Railroad at the end of the Conductor training. I am not sure they do this anymore. You will have to contact them to verify.

Recently NARS has allowed other railroad companies to come in and interview the students at the end of the school. Call and verify this!

The NARS program also offers an Associate of Science Degree in Railroad Technology.

2. https://scc.losrios.edu/railroad-operations/railroad-operations/railroad-operations
Sacramento City College offers a Certificate program in Railroad Operations. Ask them about employment assistance after graduation.

2. https://railway.broad.msu.edu/education/
Michigan State University has a program on Railway Management Certificate Program

4. https://gatewayct.edu/
Gateway Community College has programs for Associate in Science for railroad positions. Gateway is located in New Haven, CT.

5. https://catalog.coastalpines.edu/degrees?degrees_keys=locomotive
Coastal Pines Technical College in Georgia has Railroad Systems and Locomotive courses.

Always ask about job placement assistance with every school you speak with!

Here are a few other links that have railroad related trade school information:

http://www.railroaddata.com/rrlinks/Railroad_Training_Programs/

http://www.railindustry.com/index.html#sthash.LvX5tX3Y.dpbs

Remember, if your goal is to go to a trade school, check and **make sure that the program offers an interview and job placement services.** Several of the schools I listed do have an interview program and that is what you want.

Something to take into consideration with the trade schools is which railroad companies they offer interviews with. You want to make sure that they are Class One railroads which are the biggest railroads and **pay the highest rates**.

That being said they may also provide interviews with Class 2 and Class 3 railroads. If you want to work for one of them, that is an excellent situation as they are smaller and may have better schedules.

You will notice that each school charges different amounts. **Don't be fooled into thinking just because a school is more expensive or less expensive that they are better or not as good.** Call each school and speak with the person in charge and ask lots of questions.

Again, I can't stress **enough,** the **most important thing is job placement.** Make absolutely sure that the school arranges a guaranteed interview with a railroad company. None of the schools can legally guarantee you a job. However, look for the schools that have **high placement ratings**. You want a school that is tied in with a railroad company.

Now, there is also the possibility that you do not want to work for the railroad company for which the school arranges an interview. **Take the interview anyway because it will give you good experience in job interviewing with a railroad.**

Then, when you interview with the railroad where you want to work, you will have that much more experience when interviewing with your preferred railroad company.

When you interview with a railroad that the trade school sets up for you, most likely the interviewer will ask you what your score was on your final exam. **Don't bother lying** because they will probably already know your score.

When you're at your trade school, you want to score as high a score as possible because this weighs heavily during your interview with the railroad. They want those people who scored at least a 90% on the final exam.

When you're at the school, you are **there for two reasons**: Score as high as you can in the school and leave there with a job. Scoring high at these schools is not as hard as you may think. You just need to be serious about your schooling and study every night. Do your homework and **study the entire five or six weeks** that the course is long.

Stop watching TV and going out drinking during your trade school! Remember, this is a start of a new career for you and you want to create a very good impression. Nothing creates a better impression to your potential future employer than finishing in the **top of your class!**

Some questions to ask the trade schools when you call them up requesting information are:

- Do you guarantee an interview with a Class One railroad?

- With which railroad company is the interview?

- Does that **railroad typically hire new employees** from your school?

- What is the passing score in order to be considered for the interviewing railroad company?

- What is **your job placement percentage?**

- Do you offer a degree program in Railroad Technology? (This is if you are interested in obtaining this degree)

- After graduating from the training, does my training go towards college credits?

- Do you **have any past students I can call and ask** about their experience at your school?

- Do you arrange for or provide housing?

These are some questions that will help you out. Of course you will have to come up with your own questions pertaining to your own situation.

Hot tip: **During your interview**: If you have a non-stable employment background, then you really want to stress the fact that you are 100% committed to a career with the railroad and that is why you chose to go to a trade school.

For example during your interview the person interviewing may say something like, "I see you've had a number of jobs in the past. Why is that?"

A good response from you would be, "Yes, I have bounced around a little bit because I was trying to decide what I wanted to do career wise. After doing a lot of research and speaking with other people in the railroad industry, I decided I wanted a career with the railroad.

I **am 100% committed to a career with the railroad** and that is why I spent a great deal of money to put myself through this trade school and worked so hard to score highly on the final exam."

You really **must sell yourself to the interviewer** on the fact that you are committed to a new and very long (until you retire) career with the railroad. That is the reason you put yourself through a trade school.

In closing on this chapter on trade schools, I want to stress again **the importance of scoring as high as you can on your final exam**. Going to the trade school and scoring high will cover the "sin" of **job instability.**

I myself went the trade school route because of one main reason. I could have chased around the country going to job interviews with the different Class One railroads and may or may not have gotten hired.

This would have cost a lot of money driving to different states to interviews. I also would have lost time at work.

The reasons I choose to go to a trade school were **convenience and speed.** I knew if I went to a trade school that my chances of getting a job were very, very good. I was not real picky about where I wanted to work. I basically just wanted to **get a job with a Class One and start working.**

Right after I graduated from the school I was offered a job and started working. Even though the school cost me a lot of money, landing a great paying job with awesome benefits and retirement were well worth the cost of the school.

Think seriously about going to a trade school because in my opinion it is a very good route to take in securing employment within the railroad industry. It is without a doubt the fastest way to getting hired. This is why it's so important to make sure you go to a trade school that has job placement assistance. If a railroad uses that school as their primary "screening process" for hiring, then as long as you score over 90% on final exam you should get hired by that railroad.

Photo courtesy of
Jeff Moore ~ http://www.trainweb.org/mccloudrails

Chapter 6

In chapter six we will see who the Class One railroads are and where to find the Class Two and Class Three railroads.

So what is the difference between the three different classes of railroads? I am glad you asked. **The three classes are decided upon according to their annual operating revenue.** The organization that monitors and classifies each railroad is the Association of American Railroads located at http://www.aar.org.

A Class I railroad, is a railroad company that has annual revenue that exceeds 250 million dollars or more in 1991 dollars. These are the biggest railroads and naturally pay the highest salaries, hourly rates etc…

North America Class I Railroads

Amtrak	http://www.amtrak.com
Burlington Northern Santa Fe	http://www.bnsf.com
Canadian National	http://www.cn.ca/
Canadian Pacific	https://www.cpr.ca/en/
CSX	http://www.csx.com
Kansas City Southern	https://www.kcsouthern.com/en-us/
Norfolk Southern	http://www.nscorp.com
Union Pacific	http://www.up.com

The above eight railroads are the Class I railroads for the United States and Canada. Technically Amtrak is not a Class I because it is a passenger railroad and not a freight railroad; however, it does meet the other requirements for being a Class I railroad.

There are really just two main differences between working for a Class I railroad versus a Class II railroad. **The first is money.** You will make a more money working for a Class I railroad than a Class II or Class III railroad.

It does not take a rocket scientist to figure out why. Obviously larger companies can afford to pay higher wages due to higher profits.

The **second big difference is lifestyle and work environment.** You will work in a friendlier atmosphere when you work for a Class II or Class III railroad. The Class II and Class III railroads are much more family friendly and because the railroads are smaller you most likely will not be away from home as much as you will be working for a Class I railroad.

So the bottom line is if you go to work for a Class II or Class III railroad you will be **giving up some income, however, you will gain a better work environment and better hours**.

Just on a side note, some of the Class II railroads offer profit sharing, bonuses, and stock options, so in the long run the pay difference may not really exist. For example the Class One railroad I work for does not offer any of those financial benefits.

Let's take a look at the Class I railroads and make sure you check out their websites located above. Each website will pretty much answer any questions you may have about each individual railroad.

Amtrak - The word or name Amtrak is a combination of the words America, travel and track. Amtrak is an intercity passenger train created in 1971. Amtrak is an independent for-profit corporation; however, its board is entirely controlled by the U.S. government through presidential appointment and Senate confirmation.

Burlington Northern Santa Fe Railroad - BNSF is the second largest railroad in America and is the result of a merger between Burlington Northern and Atchison, Topeka and Santa Fe Railway back in 1995.

Canadian National Railway - CNR is the largest freight railroad in Canada in both track mileage and revenue. CNR also runs in the United States from the Canadian border all the way down to the Gulf of Mexico.

Canadian Pacific Railway - CPR is Canada's second largest freight railroad and has its headquarters in Calgary, Alberta. It was Canada's first transcontinental railway and also operated passenger service up until 1978 when VIA Rail took over its passenger service.

CSX Transportation - CSX is one of two Class I railroads who serve the east coast. The merging of two CSX Corporation subsidiaries; Chessie System Railway and Seaboard Coast Line Industries formed it. This is how it got its name of CSX. See their website for how they recruit.

Kansas City Southern Railway - KCS is probably the smallest of the Class I railroads operating in North America. It also owns three other railroads which are Texas Mexican Railway, Grupo Transportacion Ferroviaria Mexicana and Panama Canal Railway Co.

Norfolk Southern Railway - NS is the fourth largest railroad company in America just behind CSX in track miles. NS operates in 22 states on the east coast. NS was formed by a merger between Southern Railway Company and the Norfolk & Western Railway in 1982. Norfolk Southern has over 21,500 miles of track.

Union Pacific Railroad - UP is the largest railroad in the United States. UP covers the central and western United States. Union Pacific has 32,832 miles of track and over 48,000 employees.

Be advised that the above information may be different at time of reading due to railroad company mergers.

A Class II railroad is a railroad with annual operating revenue greater than $37.4 million but less than $433.2 million. The following is a list of some of the larger Class II railroads in North America. Be advised that what I am going to list are the four larger railroad holding companies. What this means is that they are railroad companies who own several too many different railroad companies in which they have combined to form one large conglomerate.

North America Class II (Holding) Railroads

Dakota, Minnesota and Eastern (bought by CP in 2008)
Genesee & Wyoming   http://www.gwrr.com/
RailAmerica (largest Class II)   (bought by Genesse & Wyoming)
WATCO   https://www.watco.com/service/rail/

As you go to each of the above company websites you will notice that they own many different railroad companies. Below are some of the larger Class II railroad companies that may or may not belong to one of the holding companies listed above.

Alaska Railroad   https://www.alaskarailroad.com/
Pan Am Railways   http://www.panamrailways.com/
Iowa, Chicago & Eastern Railroad (bought by CP in 2008)
Montana Rail Link   http://www.montanarail.com/

Class III railroads are any freight railroad that does not meet the requirements of a Class II railroad. These are typically your very small railroads that specialize in serving the industries in their area or state. Many of the railroad holding companies listed above own

Class II and Class III railroads and that is what makes up their parent company.

For a list of Class II and III railroads:

Class II   https://www.american-rails.com/regionals.html

Class III   https://www.american-rails.com/shortlines.html

Photo courtesy of
Rob Jacox ~ http://www.trainweb.org/westernrails/

Chapter 7

Now that we know who's who in the rail industry lets find out where we can go to see who is hiring. You can go to each company website and they all will have an "employment" section that you can click on to see if they are hiring and for what positions.

Each railroad will have their own process for hiring. Some have web based applications and post job positions on their website while others tell you what positions they have openings for and where to show up for the application process.

For your convenience I will put a hot link for the employment section of the following railroads:

North America Class I Railroads

Amtrak
https://jobs.amtrak.com/

Burlington Northern Santa Fe
https://jobs.bnsf.com/

Canadian National
https://www.cn.ca/en/careers/

Canadian Pacific

https://www.cpr.ca/en/careers

CSX

https://www.csx.com/index.cfm/working-at-csx/

Kansas City Southern

https://kcsouthern-careers.silkroad.com/

Norfolk Southern

https://jobs.nscorp.com/content/career-Paths/

Union Pacific

https://up.jobs/index.htm

If any of above links do not work then go to "home" page of railroad and look for an "employment" or "jobs" link and click it.

North America Class II Railroads

Genessee & Wyoming

https://www.gwrr.com/careers

WATCO

https://www.watcocompanies.com/careers/join/

Alaska Railroad

https://www.alaskarailroad.com/corporate/careers

Pan Am Railways

http://www.panamrailways.com/careers/

Montana Rail Link

https://www.montanarail.com/careers/

At the above websites look for an "employment" or "career" link on the home page.

The following are links on the internet to websites that specialize in railroad employment opportunities. The RRB Jobs section is incredible resource on jobs and all the different railroads at bottom of the web page!

https://www.rrb.gov/Resources/Jobs

http://www.railjobs.com/

Hot Tip: When filling out an application on the internet beware that many of the websites will "time-out" on you and your information that you just entered will not be saved. Therefore make sure that you have all your information ready before you start entering your application information.

Armed with the above information you should have more than enough to know where to go to in order to see who is hiring and for what positions.

Most railroad companies only let you interview once every six months. Therefore I would recommend that you fill out several applications for the surrounding area that you want to work.

Sometimes you may fill out an application on one of the railroad websites and get a reply back that says something like, "We are interviewing candidates more qualified at this time."

What that means is they feel that you are not someone whom they want to interview. Don't give up! Contact the person whose name is on the letter or email and ask them to re-consider. This is the time to sell yourself on the phone with that person!

This actually happened to me and I was able to get the person with whom I spoke to give me a shot at the interview and guess what... I got hired!

Had I not taken the time to look up the phone number on the company website and jumped through a few hoops to find out who I could talk to, I would have never gotten the opportunity and gotten the job.

There could be several reasons for getting a rejection letter. It also could be that the person screening applications missed something on your application, such as your trade school, etc...

Hot Tip: While we are on the subject of job hunting I want to warn you of one other item of very big importance. That is the subject of diet pills or diet formulas sold over the counter or perhaps even by prescription.

These can cause you to show up **positive** for cocaine when the railroad company does your drug screening!

I know first-hand as it happened to a friend of mine. Some of these products have a coca base or ingredient and it will cause you to test positive for cocaine.

If this happens the railroad will not even bother to listen to your excuses no matter what you say.
Another thing to stay away from is bagels or bread with poppy seeds. These can also cause you to show positive for marijuana.

Basically they will simply expel you from the hiring process and move onto the next person. You also do not want to be taking any kind of pain medication as that will also show up and then they will think you have an injury and that also will keep you from getting hired.

Railroads are very paranoid when it comes to hiring someone with a potential injury as they do not want to get sued down the road for a previous injury.

Therefore try to keep your system as clean as possible from here on out so that you do not lose a job opportunity for something that is innocent but will make you look like a liability to the railroad company.

Since we are on the subject of job hunting, I want to discuss one more aspect, and that is something the railroads have done in the past and that is furloughs. This is when the railroad slows down and they have to lay off workers.

They then lay them off according to seniority and call them back as the work picks up. This has not been done in several years and you should not have to worry about it for several reasons.

The first reason is that if it did happen you will still have the opportunity to work at a different location until you get called back to your original hiring point.

The second reason is that the railroads do not want to lose workers who are trained due to a furlough. Therefore they are coming up with programs that will still pay you even if you get furloughed.

The third reason is there is a company at https://rrtemps.com/ that specializes in railroad employees and finding them work if they are furloughed or out of work. Basically it's a temporary job agency for railroad workers.

Photo courtesy of
Richard Peters ~ http://community.webshots.com/user/foosqust

Chapter 8

Now that we have the interview process and job information we need, let us look at what your resume should look like as well as the key words you are going to want to use on your resume.

Keywords are those words railroads like to see and make your resume stand out. When a human resource person scans your resume they are looking for these kinds of keywords:

Radio	Cargo	Conductor
Diesel	Engineer	Freight
Radio Communication	Brakeman	**Shift Work**
Operating Rules	Operating Crew	Damage Books
Passenger	Railroad	Refrigeration
Safety	Security	Manager
Short line	Signal	Switch
Terminal	Timetable	Truck
Train	Transportation	Delivery
Mechanical	Construction	Work Order

Here is a list of railroad related occupations that the railroad likes to see as previous jobs or work experience:

Aircraft Mechanic/Inspector	Cargo Handler
Military	Dispatcher
Distribution Manager	Delivery Driver

Engineer	Fleet Manager
Cargo Inspector	Hazardous Material Handler
Passenger Conductor	Transportation Inspector
Railroad Employee	Shipping/Receiving Clerk
Traffic Manager	Traffic Analyst
Trainman	Travel Coordinator/Clerk
Truck Driver	Yardmaster
Prison Worker	Mill Worker
Policeman	Fireman
Construction Worker	Security Worker
Safety Manager	Instructor

Don't freak out if your past employment does not fit into one of the above fields. Remember the main thing is **stability, safety** and **shift work.**

Try to gear your resume towards those three items. I also recommend that you have a resume professionally done. It's not that expensive and can make a big difference. Before I had my resume done it was terrible. I did not even realize how bad it was until I had it done professionally.

You also want your resume to only be one page long. Two main reasons for this are:

1) You want the reader of your resume to be able to digest it quickly and easily.

2) You most likely will be pasting it into a company web page with your application and you want it short and readable.

If you have your resume professionally done, ask them to give you a normal copy in MS Word, for example, that you can print out and also get a pdf copy so that you can copy and paste or upload the electronic copy onto a railroad company website when asked for your resume during the application process online.

An electronic copy is a stripped down version of your resume with out any bold lines, extra text, etc…

You can do a search on the internet for resume writing services and find many different companies who will do a resume for you pretty inexpensively.

Some very important things to keep in mind when making a resume are the following:

Your resume must be perfect which means it is easy to read, free from grammatical errors, consistent punctuation, and have a consistent format.

Many resume websites have hundreds of templates you can use and have professional writers who can write your resume for you. They will ask you lots of different questions about your past work history, performance, etc... in order to make a resume for you that stands out from the crowd.

Here is one resume site I found: https://www.resumenerd.com/

On the next page I will post my own resume so that you can see what a resume geared towards the railroad looks like. Keep in mind that I have changed the information on my resume to keep my personal information private. My resume was geared towards getting a job as a railroad Conductor.

I found a webpage on the Union Pacific railroads website that lists all the different railroad jobs and their descriptions. This is excellent for looking up what position you are interested in working as and writing down the key words.
https://up.jobs/search-jobs.html

The most important thing you can do before writing a resume is researching the job description so that you can pick up the key words and incorporate them into your own resume.

Sample next page:

Sean Martin

---

123 Main St * Anchorage, AK 98342 * 910-555-1212 * seanmartin@yahoo.com

OBJECTIVE: A position as a Conductor in the railroad industry.

SUMMARY OF QUALIFICATIONS

- Graduate, Conductor Training Program, Mohawk Valley Community College.
- 7 years experience in transportation industry.
- One year experience as Safety Manager while in United States Marine Corps.
- Four years experience in management while at Hauer Paper Mill.

EDUCATION

Graduate, Conductor Training Program,
Mohawk Valley Community College, Utica, NY July 2003
XYZ Sales & Management Training for Sales Managers (2002)

RELEVANT EXPERIENCE AND ACCOMPLISHMENTS

Transportation, Shipping and Safety
- Drove delivery truck for Federal Express for 6 years injury free.
- Arranged all shipping and obtained new shipping accounts for Federal Express.
- Taught safety classes and conducted safety inspections as the Safety Manager in Marine Corps.
- Managed all logistics for operation Dark Frost during last year in Marine Corps.

Management
- Managed 12 employees while at Hauer Paper Mill.
- Developed and implemented Safety program for entire unit in Marine Corps.
- Won the Safety award for lowest accident rating of all departments while at Hauer Paper Mill.

Customer Service and Communication
- Provided customer service to customers while driving for Federal Express.
- Maintained excellent customer relations while at Hauer Paper Mill.
- Operated and communicated through field portable radios during field operations in Marine Corps.

WORK HISTORY

Chip Department Manager	Hauer Paper Mill	Feb. 1999 - Jun., 2003
Fed Ex Driver	Federal Express	Jan. 1993 - Feb., 1999
United States Marine Corps	USMC	Dec. 1989 - Dec., 1993

~~~~~~

This is just a sample resume and all information in the above is false. I just wanted to give you an idea how to use key words and possibly format your resume. There are several different formats you can use for a resume. A resume service will discuss these with you in order to see which one is best for your situation.

Chapter 9

In this chapter I want to give you the websites for the railroad and transportation unions you will be a part of after you get hired. The union representative will contact you after you are hired and answer any questions you may have about your particular job, etc…

I'm also going to give you websites that are important for you to look at and they will provide you with a great deal of information.

Railroad Unions and Organizations

Brotherhood of Locomotive Engineers and Trainmen
https://ble-t.org/

Smart Union (formerly United Transportation Union)
https://smart-union.org/

Brotherhood of Maintenance of Way Employees Division
https://www.bmwe.org/default.aspx

Brotherhood of Railroad Signalmen
http://www.brc.org/

Brotherhood of Railway Carmen Division (merged with IAMAW)
https://www.goiam.org/

International Association of Machinists and Aerospace Workers
https://www.goiam.org/

International Brotherhood of Electrical Workers
http://www.ibew.org/

Sheet Metal Workers International Association
https://smart-union.org/

Transport Workers Union of America
http://www.twu.org/

The following sites are also important sites for you to check out:

Railroad Workers United
http://railroadworkersunited.org/

The Federal Railroad Administration
The FRA makes up the rules and regulations that the railroad
companies must follow. It is a government agency.
https://railroads.dot.gov/

Railroad Retirement Board
The RRB will give you all the information on how railroad retirement
works, the pay and benefits.
http://www.rrb.gov/

The Association of American Railroads

http://www.aar.org/

The General Code of Operating Rules for Conductors and Engineers

http://www.trainweb.com/gcor/general.html#sthash.B73mSXlU.dpbs

The Transportation Trades Department

This is a "voice for transportation workers" website.

http://www.ttd.org/

This is a great website with over 10,000 railroad and train related links.

http://www.trainweb.org/

Railroad website with thousands of web links and a great railroad forum.

http://www.railroaddata.com/

This is another great site with rail-cams.

http://www.trainorders.com/

This is a nice site with railroad fonts, clipart, train screensavers, etc...

http://www.cwrr.com

In our next and last chapter we are going to recap everything we have learned in this book.

Photos courtesy of
Rob Jacox ~ http://www.trainweb.org/westernrails/

Chapter 10

This is the last and final chapter in our book and I hope you have learned a great deal from it. This chapter is basically going to recap what you have learned so far. After reading this book and going to all of the different resources I have shared with you, I am confident that you are 100% ready when you strike out on your venture of a brand new exciting railroad career.

In the **first chapter** we learned about what will prevent you from getting hired with the railroad industry. We also learned what the jobs consist of and in what kind of environment you will be working.

We also examined the "scary speech" and what it is used for as well as what kinds of things the railroad industry is and is not. We saw that the railroad industry is a 24/7 type of business and not for everybody. It's more of a lifestyle than anything else.

In the **second chapter**, we learned the three most important characteristics the railroad industry is looking for: Safety, Stability and Shift work.

We examined how to become a safety manager at your current employer in order to boost your resume strength and the importance of safety to the railroad industry. Safety is everything to the railroad industry. The equipment is huge, very heavy and even more unforgiving.

We saw how stability is looked on very favorably with the rail industry and how shift work can greatly boost your chances of getting hired.

We also found out the two ways railroads hire and that is straight from their own hiring sessions and through specialized railroad trade schools.

In the **third chapter** we looked at many of the different questions you may get asked at an interview session. I listed the best possible answers to those questions. Remember to gear those answers to your own situation and the type of railroad with which you are interviewing.

We also learned to do research on the railroad company you are interviewing with so that you can use their own company information to gear your answers and questions towards that individual company.

You learned how to customize your interview with each different company.

In **chapter four** we discussed the importance of having all of your information such as past employers, phone numbers, addresses, etc... available, when you fill out your applications. This is particularly important when applying online because some websites will "time out" on you and your work will be lost. That means you will end up doing it all over again.

We also discussed the good, bad, and ugly about background investigations.

I told you that anything in the public such as drivers' license records, criminal records, and education records are easily verified.

We also discussed what can and can not be verified with past employers.

In **chapter five** we discussed the advantages of trade schools and how that can make up for a history of job instability. We also found out that the fastest way to railroad employment was through a railroad trade school.

We also learned what the best questions to ask potential trade schools. The most important fact we learned about railroad trade schools is that you want to go to one that guarantees an interview with a railroad company!

In **chapter six** we looked at all of the Class I railroads as well as the larger holding companies for Class II railroads. We found out the differences in each of the classes of railroads as well as where to find out more information from each perspective railroad company.

We also learned that working for a Class I railroad will earn you a lot more money than working for a Class II railroad. However, it was noted that Class II railroads have some financial benefits not offered by most of the Class I railroad companies such as stock options, profit sharing and matching 401K programs.

In **chapter seven** we found out where to go in order to find the railroad jobs and see who is hiring. We also found out about some internet based sites that specialize in railroad jobs such as http:// www.railjobs.com and another site at https://www.rrb.gov/Resources/Jobs .

We also learned what kinds of drugs can cause you to show positive for cocaine and ruin your chances for employment. In addition we learned about furloughs in the railroad industry.

The last thing we learned about in chapter seven is what to do if you get a rejection letter or email not wanting to interview you for a railroad position.

In **chapter eight** we discussed your resume and how to make it powerful by adding the key words railroads are searching for. We found those keywords as well as previous job experience the railroads like to see.

We found out where to find job descriptions for different railroad positions at
https://up.jobs/index.htm .
.

We also saw a sample resume using key words and learned how to incorporate keywords into our resume by researching the job position we are applying for.

In **chapter nine** we found out the different union and trade related websites that are connected and represent railroad workers.

We also found other websites that are important to know and familiarize ourselves with such as the Railroad Retirement Board
http://www.rrb.gov/.

That is it for this very specialized book and I hope you enjoyed it as much as I did in researching and writing it and working in this industry as a conductor with Union Pacific.

I would really love to read your review, please go here to amazon.com and leave your review. Thank you!

If you have any questions you can also reach me in the private Facebook group here: https://www.facebook.com/groups/railroadjobs

Best Regards,

Sean Martin

Sean Martin

Ps. I want to thank the great photographers who donated the photo's I used in this book. (No particular order)

Ronal Kappel	http://www.ronaldus.com
Richard Peters	http://community.webshots.com/user/foosqust
Susan Thomas	http://community.webshots.com/user/susan526
Rob Jacox	http://www.trainweb.org/westernrails/
Jeff Moore	http://www.trainweb.org/mccloudrails